LIFE FOR US

Choman Hardi was born in Iraqi Kurdistan just before her family fled to Iran. She returned to her home town at the age of five and lived there until she was fourteen. When the Iraqi government used chemical weapons on the Kurds in 1988 her family fled to Iran again. She lived in Iraq, Iran and Turkey before coming to England in 1993.

She studied philosophy and psychology at Queen's College, Oxford and has an MA in philosophy from University College London. She recently completed doctorate research at the University of Kent in Canterbury on the mental health of Kurdish women refugees between the clash of cultures. She lives in Slough.

She has published three books of poetry in Kurdish: *Return with no memory* (Denmark, 1996), *Light of the shadows* (Sweden, 1998) and *Selected Poems* (Iraqi Kurdistan, 2003). *Life for Us* (Bloodaxe Books, 2004) is her first collection in English.

Choman Hardi was commissioned by the South Bank and Apples & Snakes to take part in Poetry International at the Royal Festival Hall in 2002, and was awarded a Jerwood-Arvon Young Poet's Apprenticeship in 2003.

She has facilitated creative writing workshops for the British Council (UK, Belgium, Czech Republic and India) as well as many other organisations. Also an artist, Choman Hardi has contributed to a number of joint exhibitions in Britain and across Europe.

She was chair of Exiled Writers' Ink!, a group of established refugee writers who write in another language as well as English. The organisation aims to represent those writers whose voice has not been represented in the main stream British media.

Her father Ahmad Hardi, who also lives in Britain, is a well-known and much respected Kurdish poet: 'Poetry started with my father, his regular recital of poetry at moments of anger, sadness, and laughter has had the greatest effect on me.'

CHOMAN HARDI

Life for Us

BLOODAXE BOOKS

ISBN: 1 85224 644 8

First published 2004 by
Bloodaxe Books Ltd,
Highgreen,
Tarset,
Northumberland NE48 1RP.

www.bloodaxebooks.com
For further information about Bloodaxe titles
please visit our website or write to
the above address for a catalogue.

Bloodaxe Books Ltd acknowledges
the financial assistance of
Arts Council England, North East.

Cover printing by J. Thomson Colour Printers Ltd, Glasgow.

Printed in Great Britain by
Cromwell Press Ltd, Trowbridge, Wiltshire.

For my scattered family
and my husband

ACKNOWLEDGEMENTS

Acknowledgements are due to the editors of the following publication where some of these poems first appeared: *Crossing the Border, Velocity, Index on Censorship, Poetry London, P.E.N. International* and *Exiled Ink!*

The following poems were commissioned by the South Bank and Apples & Snakes for the Poetry International festival in 2002: 'The weekly chicken', 'Qleeshayawa', 'Nights in the cellar', 'The middle way', 'My children', 'Somehow', 'Our doomed leaders' and 'Anfal'.

'To Kurdistan', 'Pyjamas 1983' and 'There was...' (formerly called 'Displacement') were broadcast on BBC Radio 4 in August 2003.

I'm grateful to the South Bank/Apples & Snakes project and the Jerwood-Arvon mentoring scheme for giving me the opportunity to work with Moniza Alvi and George Szirtes respectively. Both of these periods have been essential for my development as a writer. Also to the P.E.N./Arvon creative writing course for giving me the opportunity to work with Lawrence Sail.

I'm particularly grateful for the valuable feedback and support of Jane Duran, Moniza Alvi, George Szirtes and Lawrence Sail. This collection would not have been possible without their help.

Special thanks to Jennifer Langer whose dedication and hard work in founding Exiled Writers' Ink! has given me and many other writers a platform.

CONTENTS

9   There was...
10 Journey through the dead villages
11 What I want
12 One of father's absences
13 My mother's hands
14 My father's books
15 My mother's kitchen
16 Strings
17 *Qleeshayawa*
18 Nights in the cellar
19 Dropping gas: 16th March 1988
20 The spoils, 1988
21 The Penelopes of my homeland
22 Lausanne, 1923
23 My country
24 Life for us
25 Living in Saqiz
26 The weekly chicken
27 Fasting
28 The church and the mosque
29 Seeing
30 At the border, 1979
31 Escape journey, 1988
32 Invasion
33 Exodus, 1991
34 Two pages
34   1 *Delivering a message*
35   2 *Not delivering a message*
36 Three moments
36   I *Sweeping the snow*
37   II *The sunrise*
38   III *The best return*
39 The 1983 riots in Suleimanya
39   I *The arrest*
40   II *The haunting*
41   III *Pyjamas, 1983*
42 Our doomed leaders
43 Our war
44 My homeland
45 Somehow

46 Places we come from
47 His boots
48 To Kurdistan
49 The songs
50 The greening mountains
51 Summer roof
52 Extracts from an autobiography
54 One life
55 Tying the moments together
56 Opening brackets in a rush
57 What colour
58 Harmless whispers
59 Something
60 Mixed marriage
62 The middle way
63 My children
64 As your head grows heavy on my shoulder

There was...

There is a place where you can smell the satisfaction of the land
when the first rain falls, and you can hear the fat raindrops.

There is a place where it doesn't rain continuously
where you can sleep on flat roofs in the hot evenings
and it snows to let you know that another winter has arrived.

There is a house with four bedrooms
where a couple live with their three children
one of them is seven years old and the other two are three.

There was a house with four bedrooms
where seven people used to live
and they ate around a flowery sifra every day.

And a young man used to play his flute until the women cried
maybe for what there was, or for what there would be.
And a father was torn between politics and poetry.

And a little girl believed that there was a bell in her ear
and managed to avoid wearing slippers
even when the floor burnt her feet.

There was a garden where the brown chicks
would grow big enough to be killed, and every death was cried over.
Where a lonely fish was swimming aimlessly in a blue pot

and a small goat once spent a night. There was a place
before the marriages took place, before the mountains attracted
        the men
before the buying of one-way tickets

there was a place where seven people lived happily in the four
        seasons.

Journey through the dead villages

Sometimes one journey
is the beginning of a hundred journeys
each journey undoable
leading to other little journeys
each journey entailing a hundred possibilities
a hundred departures.
No journey is understood in all its aspects.

This journey started with my brother's tears.
On the fringe of our land
my brother was informed of a death.
I had never seen him cry
even returning after an absence
swollen, broken, and only seventeen
I had never seen him cry.

Within the sadness that enveloped the beginning of our journey
we left behind most of our food.
While crossing through the dry-lipped mountains
we made do with bread and water
and every meal,
when we remembered the absent food,
we remembered the absent man.

The villages we crossed were empty.
The scattered sheep without their shepherd
were circling in sadness and fear.

We crossed the forbidden border,
witnessed the scariness of silence.
Our journey stopped in this neighbouring land
where we spent four years covered up.
But that wasn't all.
Each journey entails a hundred possibilities
each undoable, leading to other little journeys.

What I want

My father never had what he wanted
and we still don't have the homeland he taught us to love.
For many years he told us off
when he became aware of our loud earrings
when we dressed in red or perfumed our hair.

He spoke of the neighbours
who were mourning the death of their sons
of the poisoned, soulless villages
of the spring of '88 which was full of death.
He spoke of the end of the bigger war
which meant further energy for destroying us.

Father cried
when he smelt the first daffodils of each spring
when he saw images of the happy children
who weren't aware of what was happening.

In his despair he kept saying:
Like the American Indians
our struggle will become a topic for films.

And I imagine what it would be like
to have what my father struggled for
and I imagine the neighbours
not visiting the graveyard in despair.

I imagine humane soldiers
soldiers who would never say:
'We will take you to a place
where you will eat your own flesh.'
And I imagine what it would be like
to have what my father struggled for.

11

One of father's absences

The second daughter remembers the day.
She always cries retelling the story
but her father does not.
He remembers many more trivial things
but however much he thinks and tries
he cannot recollect that very moment.

Even her mother doesn't.
She remembers crying and cooking him soup,
how the two men returned him, holding his armpits,
left him, convinced he was dying.

The four of them were playing in the garden,
each a year taller than the next one.
From the moment he arrived in the yard
he stared at them with his fully open eyes.
He was struggling for a breath, a word
and could only beckon them with his hand.

They stood by the wall
each trying to hide behind the others,
too shy to hold his hand or give him a kiss.

My mother's hands

When I kiss her wrinkled hands now
they smell of garlic and onion from the daily cooking.
Years ago when she was younger
and we were back home
sometimes her hands smelt of bread.

On these days she woke at sunrise
covering her forehead in a white scarf
kneading the dough until it was smooth.
We would hear the *paramez* wailing
as she pumped the oil
to stabilise the flames under the baking tray.

Then she was ready to sit on the floor
folding her right leg under her
stretching her other leg under the *pinna*.

She rocked back and forth
as the rolling pin moved under her palms
flattening the blobs of dough into nans
baked and piled in the store cupboard.
Her palms were sore and swollen for days.

Some days her hands smelt of meat.
It took her hours hand-mincing the beef.
She fried half of it with chopped onions
boiled almonds, raisins and herbs:

the other half she mixed with ground rice
to make the dough for *kifta*.
She opened the dough in the palm of her left hand
and stuffed it with the fried meat.
Fifty large *kiftas* on each occasion –
she could hardly walk after making them.

On autumn evenings when we gathered by the fire
my mother's hands smelt of orange.
It was my father's favourite fruit,
though she always had to peel it.

My father's books

It was autumn 1988
when my father's books dispersed.
One by one they came off the shelves,
cleaned themselves of his signature
and grouped, choosing different fates.

The books with conscience divided.
The stubborn ones set themselves alight,
too rebellious in their objection
they chose death over a life in the dark.

The others preferred a hiding place.
Hoping to see the light again
they packed themselves into a luggage bag,
buried themselves in the back garden,
to be recovered many years later
crumpled, eaten by the damp.

The rest chose more stable homes
where they wouldn't be abandoned again.
They shone on other people's shelves
keeping their secret to themselves.

My mother's kitchen

I will inherit my mother's kitchen.
Her glasses, some tall and lean, others short and fat,
her plates, an ugly collection from various sets,
cups bought in a rush on different occasions,
rusty pots she can't bear throwing away.
'Don't buy anything just yet,' she says,
'soon all of this will be yours.'

My mother is planning another escape,
for the first time home is her destination,
the rebuilt house which she will furnish.
At 69 she is excited about
starting from scratch.
It is her ninth time.

She never talks about her lost furniture
when she kept leaving her homes behind.
She never feels regret for things,
only for her vine in the front garden
which spread over the trellis on the porch.
She used to sing for the grapes to ripen
sew cotton bags to protect them from the bees.
I know I will never inherit my mother's trees.

Strings

From one branch of the fig tree
stretching to the window
a string made the line for our clothes

the strings we once had for swinging at picnic
used to hurt my bottom
and my mother made a special cushion for the swing –
once we hung it from the gate on a summer afternoon
and the neighbours came to have a swing too

the strings we use to tie our lives together
the strings that stretch with us
the strings that hold us back
and the strings that strangle our brothers

Roj was given back to his parents in pieces
although his sentence was to be hanged

a blue string reminds me of travelling on a spring day
watering the thirsty grass
and loving the sky
we spoke in clear blue at those times
a string was still a harmless thing.

Qleeshayawa

'*Qleeshayawa*,' they would say and start running
the old, the young, men and women.
'*Qleeshayawa*,' they would say, *it's cracking.*

The young men joked about it –
It's our marathon, it keeps us healthy.

They ran
sometimes with no expression on their faces,
other times covered with the sweat of fear
            running, looking back,
running, looking back,
or joking.

Sometimes it was triggered by a gunshot
or the sight of vicious soldiers
            jumping out from their tank into a square.
Other times, accidentally, if somebody ran
                        they all followed.

Sometimes they would be surrounded by tanks
            with nowhere to run
and forced to stand like a flock of sheep,
to witness the execution of a friend,
to clap and shout:
            Long live justice!

Nights in the cellar

Is it fireworks or fire?
This was the story every night
going down to the cellar which smelt of smoke
when red shots scratched the sky.

Once we were in the cellar
when one of the posters dropped
and the white space on the wall
showed the change in colour.

Father wondered whether my brothers smoked
Never, was always the answer.
We all knew it of course
but played the game of not knowing.

And even many years later
there was no smoking before father.
It's disrespectful, my brothers said.
Plus, he does have asthma you know.

Is it fireworks or fire?
Merely bullets cutting walls and bodies,
young bodies which we never saw
and scarred walls hidden by His pictures.

And every morning we went to school
noticing more pictures of Him,
pictures the Night-Men dared to rip off
revealing the pockmarked walls.

Is it fireworks or fire?
It was always fire down there
and mother's shivers and prayers.
She never got used to the noise.

Dropping gas: 16th March 1988

It is not quiet in Halabja, though it should be.
I return from the mountains with the rest.
What is it about wanting to know?
Wanting to see so that you believe?
What is it about not being able to just let go?

Half of the houses are still standing
and the rest, you can see what they were made of –
bricks and cement, windows and doors
flesh and blood.

There are screams and cries everywhere
of those discovering the bodies of their loved ones –
children who managed to escape their courtyards
and died outside on the steps,
a man's back and the face of his baby under his arm.

My neighbour says, *They are all dead.*
He wants to show me his family.
There are some journalists taking photos,
some men robbing the dead bodies
and a clear sky –
it's all dead now, cannot be killed any more.

I stand detached from everything,
observing, believing and not believing.
My neighbour will lose his mind and kill himself next week,
a woman who does not find her daughter
will search for her till the day she dies,
the man who left his family behind
will live in a hell of his own
and the Imam who always called for prayers
will soon take to drink.

I stand here watching, crying and not crying.
I know that I don't know anything,
that I will never know anything
and I know that this ruin
is the only knowledge I will ever have.

The spoils, 1988
(for the 182,000 victims of Anfal, Kurdistan, Iraq)

Anfal came!
The little sparrows stopped practising their first flight.
The sheep died drinking from the water they trusted.
The caves were choked in gas.
The houses were flattened.

The villagers were taken, separated,
those who cried were shot because they cried,
those who didn't were shot because they didn't.
They were kept in the southern sands.
Those who survived the desert
were buried together, alive.

Anfal came!
The soldiers spoke a foreign language.
The villagers thought they were Muslim brothers
but they spat at the Qura'an the imams held before them,
pissed on the engraved name of Allah,
bulldozed the village mosques.

Anfal came and some survived it.
Of those who survived
some went back and rebuilt their houses.
They washed the roads, perfumed the air,
replanted the trees.

Some couldn't bear to return.
They left for unknown destinations
and started their lives in a new land
speaking in a foreign language.
They got remarried, had new children, found jobs,
laughed and danced as before.

But sometimes, on very hot days
when the land smelt a particular way
listening to music
they would remember Anfal.

The Penelopes of my homeland

(for the 50,000 widows of Anfal)

Years and years of silent labour
the Penelopes of my homeland
wove their own and their children's shrouds
without a sign of Odysseus returning.

Years and years of widowhood they lived
without realising, without ever thinking
that their dream was dead the day it was dreamt,
that their colourful future was all in the past,
that they had lived their destinies
and there was nothing else to live through.

Years and years of avoiding despair, not giving up,
holding on to hopes raised by palm-readers,
holding on to the wishful dreams of the nights
and to the just God
who does not allow such nightmares to continue.

Years and years of raising more Penelopes and Odysseuses
the waiting mothers of my homeland grew old and older
without ever knowing that they were waiting,
without ever knowing that they should stop waiting.

Years and years of youth that was there and went unnoticed
of passionate love that wasn't made
of no knocking on the door after midnight
returning from a very long journey.

The Penelopes of my homeland died slowly
carrying their dreams into their graves,
leaving more Penelopes to take their place.

Lausanne, 1923

Sitting around an old table
they drew lines across the map
dividing the place
I would call my country.

My country

I carry it in my handbag every day
in books about genocide –
pictures of mass graves, of leaders hanged,
children mutilated by chemical weapons.

I carry it in my memories of levelled villages,
cemented springs, polluted land,
in all the cancers, miscarriages, sterility.

I sing my country for the silence that surrounds it.
I remember a country forgotten
by everyone else.

Life for us

In Qala-Chwalan,
in a holiday cottage with a courtyard
and a large swimming pool –
we watched the men undress,
dive into the water, get out,
drink a glass of cold beer,
have a few spoons of beans and salad
then dive in again,
making enormous splashes as they swam.

And we,
fully dressed in the hot summer afternoon,
could tuck up our dresses
and dangle our feet in the water.

My male cousins, as young as I was
kept arguing:
Being a boy is better than being a girl
and doesn't swimming prove this?

The liquid round my ankles seduced me.
Fully dressed, I jumped in the pool
and held on to the slippery side bars.

I loved the gentle embrace of water,
reducing the warmth of the sun.
It must have felt the same inside my mother,
simple and relaxing.

I became braver, let go of the bar,
but the next moment I was drowning,
my colourful clothes holding me down.
For a slight second as I plummeted
I saw my clothes spreading out
like petals, opening up in all directions.

Living in Saqiz

The women looked as if they were mourning.
Scarves, *manto*, trousers, shoes
and even socks were black and brown.
But when they got home
they changed into their bright Kurdish outfits,
showed off their cleavages,
enhanced their curves
and put on their loose, see-through scarves.

What I miss is the calmness of summer evening –
the slow pace of life, chatting on the grass,
eating melon, drinking iced water.
And the park that people escaped to,
where the young men found their future wives –
girls wrapped up like presents, waiting,
showing off a few strands of hair.

The weekly chicken

Dividing the chicken was never easy –
deciding which part goes to who!
One chicken for a large family.

The breast was cut into two pieces:
half of it was given to my father
and the other half divided in two,
each quarter for one of my brothers.

One thigh was given to my mother,
the other divided between my aunts,
then we, the children, were given the wings
ribcage and the back, the size of the pieces
reflecting our ages – we were never happy.

Dividing the chicken wasn't easy.
My mother always avoided the task:
my aunt Roonak struggled with it.

Fasting

Those hot days of thirst
when the sun seemed to take years to set
the steady heat made you sweat
depriving you of the little water you kept.

Those long middays
when you would faint before a fan
which merely stirred the warm air.
When you had to keep up the routine of praying,
of washing your hands, feet and forehead.
When you rinsed your stale mouth five times
but always spat the water out to the last bit.

When, with your sticky throat, you craved,
craved the cool liquid to gulp down.
When you sat with your head covered at sunset,
facing Mecca, waiting for the Imam's permission.
When you sat next to a bucket of iced water,
a steel glass which hissed
as it reached your feverish lips.

The church and the mosque

Somebody asked me:
When did you first enter a church?

My philosophy tutor would argue:
It is a moot question!
Would it be cogent to reply:
When I was five years old
in a white dream?

But I was 18 and the church was poor.
The most beautiful church in town
was converted into a mosque, you see.
Yet my mother is so comfortable with her culture.

We always argue, her and me,
we always argue.
But it is all undone with a smile and a wink
unlike the bits that were added to the church.

Seeing

Life is by invitation, somebody once told me,
and seeing depends on the spectacles you wear.

A man is walking down the street
wearing glasses and led by a dog.
Whenever he hears a familiar 'hello'
he smiles kindly and lifts his hat.

I do know the meaning of 'pink', he says,
I associate it with that wonderful feeling of loving her,
with the tender touch of the back of her neck
and the calm perfume she sometimes wears.

My neighbour is obsessed with visiting the optician,
he keeps taking his children too.
He's always checking the simple facts
in case things are happening behind his back.

And a young couple argue on the street.
You're being paranoid, she shouts in his face,
I touched his hand by accident... by accident.

A man stabs his brother to death
thinking he is the enemy.

I drop my father's glasses and prepare
to see things that weren't visible to him,
feeling freed from the distortions.

But suddenly
my own reflection in the window stops me.

At the border, 1979

'It is your last check-in point in this country!'
We grabbed a drink –
soon everything would taste different.

The land under our feet continued
divided by a thick iron chain.

My sister put her leg across it.
'Look over here,' she said to us,
'my right leg is in this country
and my left leg in the other.'
The border guards told her off.

My mother informed me: *We are going home.*
She said that the roads are much cleaner
the landscape is more beautiful
and people are much kinder.

Dozens of families waited in the rain.
'I can inhale home,' somebody said.
Now our mothers were crying. I was five years old
standing by the check-in point
comparing both sides of the border.

The autumn soil continued on the other side
with the same colour, the same texture.
It rained on both sides of the chain.

We waited while our papers were checked,
our faces thoroughly inspected.
Then the chain was removed to let us through.
A man bent down and kissed his muddy homeland.
The same chain of mountains encompassed all of us.

Escape Journey, 1988

They force you to crawl, these mountains,
even if you are only 14.
Who made the first journey over them?
Whose feet created this track?

The exhausted mules carry us
along with the smuggled goods.
Sitting on their backs, climbing mountains
feels much safer than going down.
The steepness makes me lean backwards,
my back nearly touching the mule's,
then holding on becomes impossible
and I dismount.
It is easier, safer to walk sideways.

And from high up, I can see the white valley.
'A valley of plaster,' I tell my sister.
The mule owner says: 'It is snow.'
But I cannot imagine being rescued from this rough mountain
only to walk over the snow, covering the river.
I cannot imagine listening to the rushing water
passing by holes where the river exposes itself.

'You are too young to complain,'
the mule owner says,
and I look at my father, his little body,
and listen to his difficult breathing.
But then again, he's been here before.

Invasion

Soon they will come. First we will hear
the sound of their boots approaching at dawn
then they'll appear through the mist.

In their death-bringing uniforms
they will march towards our homes
their guns and tanks pointing forward.

They will be confronted by young men
with rusty guns and boiling blood.
These are our young men
who took their short-lived freedom for granted.

We will lose this war, and blood
will cover our roads, mix with our
drinking water, it will creep into our dreams.

Keep your head down and stay in doors –
we've lost this war before it has begun.

Exodus, 1991

They came three months after the uprising.
Their heels were attached to loudspeakers,
their sound reached us miles before they did.
The rumour of their brutality reached us
how they raped children, killed the bedridden.
We took to the mountains with our blankets and bread.

Our towns remained unshaken.
The soldiers were received by ghostly streets
dark houses and a monotonous, cold rain.

Two pages

1 *Delivering a message*

I was asleep in the middle of a pad
when he started writing on the first page.
The tip of his pen pressed down
forcing pale words into the pages below.
He wrote many versions that night
some very lengthy, others brief.

When my turn came he paused,
palmed his temples, squeezed his eyes,
made himself a calming tea.

She received me early one morning
in a rush, leaving her flat.
She ripped the envelope. Then, gradually,
her steps slowed down,
her fingers tightened around me.

2 Not delivering a message

All my life I waited for words –
a poem, a letter, a mathematical puzzle.

On March 16th 1988
thousands of us were taken on board –
you can't imagine our anticipation.

When they threw us out from high above
we were confused, lost in blankness.
All those clean white pages
parachuting into town...

Puzzled faces looked up
expecting a message, but we were blank.

Two hours later they dropped the real thing.
We had been testing the wind direction.
Thousands of people were gassed that day.

Three moments

I *Sweeping the snow*

There you were
sweeping the snow from the flat roof.
With your plastic spade
you pushed it to the edge
until it tumbled down
drowning the garden in waves.

Then you would come down
and mother would give you a heated cloth
to warm your hands.
Don't hold your hands up to the fire,
she would say, *they will ache.*
And I would make you a cup of tea.

*It's good having children so late
dad never needs to bother with the snow.*
But mum always bothered with things
and she still does.
Soon afterwards you too were gone
and I was alone to watch our parents grow old.

I bare my feet to touch the dew in the field.
The birds have just woken up singing
calling the sleepy sun to rise,
the same sunrise our father spoke about.
Do you remember?
We imagined his waking at dawn
running to the top of the hill
inhaling the sleepy beams of the sun
feeling hopeful, strong, happy.

And here I am, walking towards the same spring
which you said was capable of freezing a hand
held in there long enough.

I wonder whether the greenness will swallow me again!
You knew there was a ditch
covered with floating watercress
but you didn't tell me until I was in it
and you were laughing.
It is another story to tell your children, you said
but I wasn't happy. For the next few days
the skin on my legs was rough and peeling.

The spring is as cold as you said it was
and strong enough to push my hand back.
I touch the clear pebbles at the bottom.
Gently the sun emerges and I look away.
There are hills and mountains at the horizon
yellow, orange, and light purple
and the same question comes to my mind.
Why does the sunrise resemble the sunset?
And again, you're not able to tell me.

III *The best return*

My mother tells me
to dream of fish is a good thing –
each fish is a wish come true.

I arrive in the timid spring rain.
You greet me with a hug,
wearing a suit and not smoking.

You are as lean as you used to be
as I always remember you.
Your straight brown hair falls on your forehead
dry and beautiful.

We talk very little but we smile.
You are still wearing the same pair of glasses
the chunky black frame we laughed about:
Like those worn by school inspectors.

We casually wait in a train station.
Now you are a father of three,
the son our father dreamt about.

Under the rail-tracks a river flows –
clean water and fully see-through,
the colourful fish swimming up and down.

Some wet sparrows are singing somewhere
and we sit waiting, watching the fish
smiling at those timid drops of rain.

The 1983 riots in Suleimanya

I *The arrest*

Just home from school, I remember the phone call.
My mother was about to serve lunch.

I remember her face wrinkling,
her voice dropping, becoming strange
and tears rolling, rolling, rolling down her cheeks.

She was making strange sounds, not really screams,
not really cries, just strange sounds.

They will kill him, she kept saying.
He will die a horrible death.

A few minutes later we were in a taxi
my mother weeping, urging the driver to get there fast.

When we got there
the whole neighbourhood was in *pura* Roonak's house,
pura Sabih was bleeding.
She had begged the soldiers not to take him,
she'd tried to kiss their boots, they beat her:
'They took him from my hands *baji*
I couldn't protect him', she said.

For years later *pura* Sabih recalled that look on his face –
When the soldiers started beating her
he'd tried to interfere,
one of them smashed his face with the butt of a gun,
that last look of a terrified man, bleeding, hopeless
only seventeen.

II *The haunting*

The same images haunted my mother every night –
being hung by his wrists which were tied behind him
when the fat flies that he hated
drank from his young blood.
Their buzzing made her furious.

He was back, swollen
with blue fingernails
and an open wound on his left temple.

He'd never be the same as before
but he was back.
Many of them never returned.

III *Pyjamas, 1983*

That year pyjamas were potential life-savers.
When the rioting students were attacked
they dispersed into the tiny roads they knew too well
and entered the first open door on their path
which was shut behind them immediately.
They wore pyjamas, drank a glass of water,
picked up a book
and pretended to be the sons of the family.

Then, there was solidarity amongst our people:
it was 'Us' versus 'Them', things were black and white
unlike now when we're being oppressed by us
even though there is no 'Them'.

Our doomed leaders

Recalling the promised springs
in this cold winter, the curse rises to my lips –

Ba le dozexda bisute ewey dengi emey sutand.
Ba le mihnetda bigawze ewey chawi emey frand.

He in whom we had hope stuffed our vision in his bag,
the vivid colours of our world slipped into his deep pockets.

He in whom we had hope took our voice with him
and marched towards the future.

He had promised to bring new colours to our land.

Unknown to us
the blueness of water said goodbye to him
the sparrows framed him with their song
the butterflies of death flew around his head.

Our war

Everything was destroyed by others
and we destroyed what they left behind –
I killed your noon, you killed my night.

I don't remember what others kept
but I remember you withholding a drop of the rain
which could have cured me.

I don't remember what others said
but I clearly remember your words
when you killed my lips.

I can't remember what others took
but I remember your stealing my eyes
and hiding them in a tin full of darkness.

Because everyone was others I forgot
but because you were me I could not.

My homeland

It is dry this land!
No generous spring or summer rains.
And the mountains, can you see?
Some are of sand,
some of the peaks as rough as rock.

I can imagine the light green shades
with a few patches of dark green
forming under the spring rain.

Yes and last year
even the spas were exhausted.
It kept raining where I was
and somebody said
we should email the rain.

It is dry this land!
The seeds have a hard life down here.
Surviving the tough seasons of thirst
needs much more than determination.

Like the people of this land
the seeds just make it to the greenness,
they just manage to see the light.

Somehow

We are in France, driving through
fields robbed by the harvest.
Only the sunflowers are still standing,
tall and full of seeds.

We walk around a lake hand in hand,
get to the huskier parts of a forest,
show the cows affection
and help a beetle back on her feet.

It is so soothing here – the soft sprinklers
everywhere. But it is the rough roads
of my childhood that I miss most, the piercing
wind, the summer earth burning my bare feet.

Places we come from

They haunt us, appear in our dreams,
forever tempting us to go back
only to drive us away when we get there.

We think we've escaped them –
scarred walls, crossed-out graffiti,
the numerous statues of the past leader,

the mourning women with unshaved legs,
unshaped eyebrows and ashy lips.

His boots

The old woman will always keep those boots.
On the day when things were ending
she was leaning on her stick, in disbelief,
when a car with black windows slowed down.

She watched the back window open fast,
and there he was, the dictator,
suddenly looking old and frail,
dropping his military boots,
replacing them with old men's shoes.

Then the window closed and the car took off
leaving dust on the pair of boots
still warm and moist from his feet.

To Kurdistan

It's June 2003. The war is over, I'm going home.
There are no direct flights yet.
I will go to a bordering country and cross over.

I buy handbags full of little jewellery for my nieces
T-shirts and shorts for my nephews
gold earrings for my sisters in law
two books and a dress for my sister
lipstick, nail varnish, perfume and jewellery
for friends who may remember me from secondary school
for old neighbours, distant relatives.

I prepare to go home every day,
can't sleep without dreaming of border guards.
I wish I could brings some books back
then I remember all the Kurdish alphabet books
that were torn and trodden-on at that border.
You teach your children Kurdish in the West.
That is where the problem lies,
you teach your children Kurdish.

I will take the repeated advice
and will not say 'to Kurdistan', when asked where I am going.
I will save myself the humiliation of being taken to the world map
and asked, 'Could you show me where that is on the map?
I don't remember having heard of it.'

The songs

These are the songs which were played
in the background of our days
in the taxis and shops
in every house we set foot in.

These are the songs
that suddenly disappeared from our lives
or we disappeared from them
when we left our homeland behind.

We carried them in our memories
and sang them on family occasions
to remember those days when things were beginning
when we were full of timid dreams
when we were in love, passionately in love
but didn't know with whom.

Fifteen years later I go to a music shop in my hometown
searching for what displacement once took from me.
The shopkeeper smiles,
'They're old songs,' he says,
not knowing how for me they never grew old.
I wasn't there when the process took place.

I listen to them in my room in Britain
and remember that spring when they were first played.
I remember being fourteen years old
an exhibition full of disturbing images
the bearded artist top to toe in black.
At that age I knew what it meant
for a brother to survive the other's hanging.

My husband says: they are nice songs.
He says he likes listening to them.

The greening mountains

What was once here is now gone.
Those nights I knew nothing of the real story
I just loved the gleam on the mountains
as if thousands of lights were turned on for a feast.

Each light was a flaming tree.
Each night another strip of the mountain was set alight,
the fire tightening like a belt:
into the deepest wrinkles it went, leaving nothing but ashes.

My father knew. His grief was endless at the sight.
My parents whispered to each other about these things.
I was kept in the dark about what they thought.

The trees were guilty
of making this landscape a little cooler and more beautiful.
They were guilty of becoming a resting place
for the men who only came down at night.

Fifteen years later here I am
in this house which has lost its past,
has no resemblance to what it was.
I have the same view of the mountain.

Now the trees are growing back.
Soon they will cover the mountains again.

Summer roof

Every night that summer
when we went to bed on the flat roof,
I stayed awake
watching the opposite roof
where he was,
a tiny light turning on
every time he puffed his cigarette.

Once I was shown his paintings
and I went home
and wrote his name all over my books.

I kept imagining what he would say,
how I would respond.
I imagined being married to him,
looking after him when he fell ill,
cooking for him and washing his hair.
I imagined sleeping on the same roof.

A whole year went by and we never talked
then suddenly an empty house opposite us,
an empty roof, not staring back
and sleepless nights for me.

Years later we met again
the same man with a few fingers missing,
bad tempered, not able to paint.

We never spoke,
we remained on our separate roofs.

Extracts from an autobiography

I said 'No' and his arm,
his strong, loving arm,
went hard and cold under my neck.
He disappeared into the darkness
and left me full of darkness.

I think of him, of his darkness,
and the rain seems to carry on forever.
Nothing seems to stop this silence,
no phone ringing to convey kisses,
no colourful letters warming my hands,
not even a fight bringing new thoughts.
How can I ever forget his eyes?

* * *

The windows are flooding with light,
bright patches of sun on the floor,
the smell of books.

Somebody rushes out of the room,
two people kiss,
and nobody knows whether the season has ended.

* * *

I carry this confusion in my womb.
Who planted the light-seeds in the garden?
Whose voice is echoing in the darkness?

My face is fading in the mirror
and I walk on the verge of darkness
carrying the confusion in my womb.

* * *

Amongst words that cry for expression
and voices that won't be silenced,
here, on this unpredictable land,
I stand before uncertainty.

Can confidence arise out of confusion?
Somebody says: listen to the little voice.

* * *

When the rain stopped I knew it was close –
there was no way back.
I put my hand in the soil and killed the little seed.
My dreams became full of infants
struggling to be born
and my mother said:
If you were pregnant
it would've been two months old now
two months old
two months
two...

* * *

Nothing can stop the flowers from bleeding any more,
nothing can stop the infants crying over their own deaths,
nothing will end this autumn vision.

* * *

I watch the season grow old.
The light trembles in the mirror.
It's so silent, the little voice won't talk to me.
I am expecting a letter
and what would be your dream for the new year?

* * *

Two deaths rushed past in thirty days.
It's still autumn and I stand rootless.
Two deaths rushed past.

I watch the leaves fall and empty the frames.
Little is left after the wind.
And I ask somebody: *Why in autumn?*
But I know I shouldn't be asking questions any more.
I received the expected letter.
I will wait for the season to take its turn
I will wait until the leaves settle down
I will wait until the little voice sings again.
Some light might be born out of this.

One life

I

12th of November
a child dies inside a woman
a woman dies inside a child
the night slips between a woman and a child.

A woman lights a candle for her child's death
a child who stopped before it ever started.
The woman and her child stare at each other
they will never start talking.

12th of November, one life is terminated
somebody cries and somebody never forgives

12th of November.

II

As I open my eyes
I know it's not there any more.
I'm as empty as my town when life fled.

As a void, I face the mirror
And see it clearly –
a little hope is miscarried
and my hands start weeping.

Tying the moments together

I'm listening to the wind,
I'm listening to the mournful wind.
The window is trembling
and sometimes crying.
The door is so still, the door is so locked
and my mother still cries over her first born
who was 'too perfect' to live.

I'm listening to the wind
and the train never stops here.
How can I ever leave this place?
The train never stops
and the wind never stops
and how can I ever tell my mother
that she might soon
cry over her last born?
I'm listening to the wind.

Opening brackets in a rush

With my back to the sun
I sit and think about the shadows.

The young woman sitting opposite me
keeps searching her bag and emptying her pockets.
Then she is looking under the table,
under the heavy wooden chair
and the papers which are three days old.

And I keep thinking we can spend a lifetime searching
for a lost something we will never find.

My train comes and leaves and here I stay
sitting, staring, thinking slowly
and opening brackets in the rush.

(It was another hot summer evening
my brother played his violin in the garden
and the passers-by stopped and clapped.

And we spent night after night
listening to his music and the frogs singing,
listening to his music and the foxes coming into town,
his music and the owls, his music and the crickets.)

The young woman sitting opposite me
gives up searching, she gives up drinking her coffee
and suddenly leaves.

I will take the next train in three minutes,
I will make it home before the dark.

What Colour?

Where do I put my love for him?
What do I name it?

Not red like the love we know
not pink like love for a friend
not white like love for a brother
more green than love for those we've grown with
less fiery than passion.

How do I express it?
And would he understand
that I crave for his warmth
yet wont let it touch me?

What colour is this strange feeling?

It is bluey tinged with green?
Is it orange running towards red?
Is it purple with a bit of white?
So mixed and difficult to understand,
what do I call this?

It maybe all the colours I feel and know,
all the shades that I love and I don't.

What do I call this? Where do I leave it?
And what can I do with all the shades he brings with him?

I must learn to be more brown
as brown as the patient soil.

Harmless whispers

The train departs leaving the late passenger behind.
Light slides on the railway. Little blossoms fall.
A girl weeps leaning on the moving window,
nobody dares to see. And the story ends,
I don't want to love again.

Light keeps travelling on the railway.
The smell of men. Little pangs in the stomach
every time that voice answers the phone.
And I know how they feel,
those who phone us only to hung up.

The streets are stained with light. Who passed from here?
Whose shopping basket was leaking today?
Tell the prophet there is no point in coming this way,
we lost our clarity too young.

Maybe next time autumn can be celebrated.
Maybe next time we can sit down and cry from happiness.
Maybe we can, maybe we will.

The train leaves the late passenger behind
and takes the crying one along.
It was all true what they said:
It always starts with harmless whispers.
I don't want to love again.

Something

Behind the calm face of silence
something is left,
something which can't be rescued anymore
or even expressed.

Behind the words and the limits of hope
it lies unsaid.
Beyond the pains it once caused,
memories and smiles it brought,
a faint something is still left.

I hold on to silence and have faith in time
hoping it will cease.
Then maybe I can laugh or maybe I can cry,
or maybe I can write myself a letter
announcing the end.
Then maybe I can cry or laugh.

Mixed Marriage

We have to buy the rings this morning.
My sisters are disappointed with me.
They keep saying:
We don't even have our own country
and your children will not care.
You are melting into other cultures.
My sisters believe I've betrayed everything.

My father is silent. My mother is crying.
When I leave the house, she says
Wear something blue for the time being
be protected from the evil eye.

* * *

DAY 1

We move in at 9.30 on Friday evening
and take bits and pieces in a taxi.
There is no electricity in the house
and he flicks a switch and then there is light.

We sleep on the carpet spreading the double duvet
and covering ourselves in the single one
and he says to me:
'Don't you think this carpet is pornographically red?'
We cuddle up giggling.

* * *

DAY 2

He has gone to bring cups and plates..
Two men arrive with our bed in pieces.
One of them leaves but comes back later.
So much hammering in the bedroom
they are both sweating.

The walls brighten up as I clean the kitchen.

The men ask me to sign a paper
and I feel guilty for not having cups
to offer them tea, or even water.

He comes home in the dark, bright and smiley.
He's brought some food and we eat on the floor.
We share the cider in a glass
we think the bed is strong enough to share our bodies.

* * *

DAY 3

The fridge and the sofa-bed are dumped down.
I struggle ripping the boxes apart.
The sofa-bed needs two people.
I cook and wait

He returns full of smiles.
I show him the new things and we kiss.
He sees the rice
and the onions and potatoes for *shiley patata*
then winks and says:
'You've done shopping for yourself then!'
I pretend to be upset. We hug.

The sofa-bed needs a lot of work.
The diagrams are confusing.
I bend to check the bottom of the frame
and he watches me and says calmly:
'Do you remember that evening in the field?'

We eat and he tells me the news.
There is war in some part of the world.
Signing the petitions did not help.
Somewhere, people are fleeing again.
We hug and I cry. Somewhere
there is another war to be remembered by children.

The Middle Way

He describes the house as a maze
which she imagines getting lost in.
The bedrooms distant from each other,
long corridors and four toilets.
'Space enough for privacy,' he says
and she imagines feeling lonely.

She describes her toilets for him:
'No comfy seats where you can sit and read.
They're on the ground
and you have to squat and push.'

He's seen some in old French houses,
and thought they were disgusting.
They disagree about hygiene –
for him it is bathing every morning,
for her it's washing your bottom after poo.

They disagree about touching.
'Men are not supposed to hug,' he says.
That's crazy, she thinks.

He was born into his own bedroom
prepared months in advance
while she slept in her parents' room
until she was eleven.
For their children they agree
to find the middle way.

My children

I can hear them talking, my children
fluent English and broken Kurdish.

And whenever I disagree with them
they will comfort each other by saying:
Don't worry about mum, she's Kurdish.

Will I be the foreigner in my own home?

As your head grows heavy on my shoulder

Every night when we go to bed,
when your breath slowly clouds my chest,
I wish I could stop thinking of tomorrow's chores
and yesterday's pain.

I wish I could freeze my thoughts on you –
sleeping peacefully on my numb arm
the corner of your mouth gently leaking
creating a pool below the collar bone.